VIOLIN

The BIG BOOK of
violin songs

ISBN 978-1-4234-2670-7

HAL•LEONARD®

Contact Us:
Hal Leonard
7777 West Bluemound Road
Milwaukee, WI 53213
Email: info@halleonard.com

In Europe contact:
Hal Leonard Europe Limited
Distribution Centre, Newmarket Road
Bury St Edmunds, Suffolk, IP33 3YB
Email: info@halleonardeurope.com

In Australia contact:
Hal Leonard Australia Pty. Ltd.
4 Lentara Court
Cheltenham, Victoria, 3192 Australia
Email: info@halleonard.com.au

CONTENTS

ALL MY LOVING
from A HARD DAY'S NIGHT

VIOLIN

Words and Music by JOHN LENNON
and PAUL McCARTNEY

ALL THE SMALL THINGS

VIOLIN

Words and Music by TOM DE LONGE
and MARK HOPPUS

ALLEY CAT

VIOLIN

By FRANK BJORN

ANOTHER ONE BITES THE DUST

Violin

Words and Music by
JOHN DEACON

AMERICA
from the Motion Picture THE JAZZ SINGER

VIOLIN

Words and Music by
NEIL DIAMOND

ANY DREAM WILL DO

from JOSEPH AND THE AMAZING TECHNICOLOR® DREAMCOAT

Violin

Music by ANDREW LLOYD WEBBER
Lyrics by TIM RICE

BE TRUE TO YOUR SCHOOL

VIOLIN

Words and Music by BRIAN WILSON
and MIKE LOVE

BAD DAY

VIOLIN

Words and Music by
DANIEL POWTER

D.S. al Coda

CODA

BARELY BREATHING

VIOLIN

Words and Music by
DUNCAN SHEIK

15

To Coda ⊕

3

D.S. al Coda

CODA

(It's A)
BEAUTIFUL MORNING

VIOLIN

Words and Music by FELIX CAVALIERE
and EDWARD BRIGATI, JR.

BEAUTY AND THE BEAST

from Walt Disney's BEAUTY AND THE BEAST

Violin

Lyrics by HOWARD ASHMAN
Music by ALAN MENKEN

Moderately slow

BEYOND THE SEA

VIOLIN

Words and Music by CHARLES TRENET,
ALBERT LASRY and JACK LAWRENCE

BLACKBIRD

VIOLIN

Words and Music by JOHN LENNON
and PAUL McCARTNEY

BLUE SUEDE SHOES

VIOLIN

Words and Music by
CARL LEE PERKINS

BOOGIE WOOGIE BUGLE BOY

from BUCK PRIVATES

VIOLIN

Words and Music by DON RAYE
and HUGHIE PRINCE

THE BRADY BUNCH

Theme from the Paramount Television Series THE BRADY BUNCH

VIOLIN

Words and Music by SHERWOOD SCHWARTZ
and FRANK DEVOL

BUTTERFLY KISSES

VIOLIN

Words and Music by BOB CARLISLE
and RANDY THOMAS

BREAKING FREE
from the Disney Channel Original Movie HIGH SCHOOL MUSICAL

VIOLIN

Words and Music by
JAMIE HOUSTON

CABARET

from the Musical CABARET

Words by FRED EBB
Music by JOHN KANDER

VIOLIN

CALIFORNIA DREAMIN'

VIOLIN

Words and Music by JOHN PHILLIPS
and MICHELLE PHILLIPS

CANDLE IN THE WIND

VIOLIN

Words and Music by ELTON JOHN
and BERNIE TAUPIN

Slow 2

CHIM CHIM CHER-EE

from Walt Disney's MARY POPPINS

Words and Music by RICHARD M. SHERMAN
and ROBERT B. SHERMAN

Violin

Lightly, with gusto

small notes optional

CLOCKS

VIOLIN

Words and Music by GUY BERRYMAN, JON BUCKLAND,
WILL CHAMPION and CHRIS MARTIN

(They Long to Be)
CLOSE TO YOU

VIOLIN

Lyric by HAL DAVID
Music by BURT BACHARACH

COLORS OF THE WIND
from Walt Disney's POCAHONTAS

VIOLIN

Music by ALAN MENKEN
Lyrics by STEPHEN SCHWARTZ

COME FLY WITH ME

VIOLIN

Words by SAMMY CAHN
Music by JAMES VAN HEUSEN

Moderate Swing

COPACABANA
(At the Copa)
from Barry Manilow's COPACABANA

Violin

Music by BARRY MANILOW
Lyric by BRUCE SUSSMAN and JACK FELDMAN

DO-RE-MI

from THE SOUND OF MUSIC

Lyrics by OSCAR HAMMERSTEIN II
Music by RICHARD RODGERS

Violin

DO WAH DIDDY DIDDY

Violin

Words and Music by JEFF BARRY
and ELLIE GREENWICH

(Sittin' On)
THE DOCK OF THE BAY

VIOLIN

Words and Music by STEVE CROPPER
and OTIS REDDING

DON'T BE CRUEL
(To a Heart That's True)

VIOLIN

Words and Music by OTIS BLACKWELL
and ELVIS PRESLEY

DON'T LET THE SUN GO DOWN ON ME

VIOLIN

Words and Music by ELTON JOHN
and BERNIE TAUPIN

DON'T SPEAK

VIOLIN

Words and Music by ERIC STEFANI
and GWEN STEFANI

41

D.S. al Coda

CODA

small notes optional

DRIFT AWAY

VIOLIN

Words and Music by
MENTOR WILLIAMS

DUKE OF EARL

VIOLIN

Words and Music by EARL EDWARDS,
EUGENE DIXON and BERNICE WILLIAMS

THEME FROM E.T. (THE EXTRA-TERRESTRIAL)

from the Universal Picture E.T. (THE EXTRA-TERRESTRIAL)

VIOLIN

Music by
JOHN WILLIAMS

Energetically

Broadly

Tempo I

EDELWEISS

from THE SOUND OF MUSIC

VIOLIN

Lyrics by OSCAR HAMMERSTEIN II
Music by RICHARD RODGERS

EVERY BREATH YOU TAKE

VIOLIN

Music and Lyrics by
STING

EVERYTHING IS BEAUTIFUL

VIOLIN

Words and Music by
RAY STEVENS

FALLIN'

VIOLIN

Words and Music by
ALICIA KEYS

FIELDS OF GOLD

VIOLIN

Music and Lyrics by
STING

FLY LIKE AN EAGLE

VIOLIN

Words and Music by
STEVE MILLER

Moderately, in 2

FOR ONCE IN MY LIFE

VIOLIN

Words by RONALD MILLER
Music by ORLANDO MURDEN

FOREVER YOUNG

VIOLIN

Words and Music by ROD STEWART,
JIM CREGAN, KEVIN SAVIGAR and BOB DYLAN

Driving beat

FUN, FUN, FUN

VIOLIN

Words and Music by BRIAN WILSON
and MIKE LOVE

Bright Rock

THE GIRL FROM IPANEMA
(Garôta de Ipanema)

VIOLIN

Music by ANTONIO CARLOS JOBIM
English Words by NORMAN GIMBEL
Original Words by VINICIUS DE MORAES

Bossa Nova

GOD BLESS THE U.S.A

VIOLIN

Words and Music by
LEE GREENWOOD

GONNA BUILD A MOUNTAIN

from the Musical Production STOP THE WORLD – I WANT TO GET OFF

Violin

Words and Music by LESLIE BRICUSSE
and ANTHONY NEWLEY

Moderately bright

GOODBYE YELLOW BRICK ROAD

VIOLIN

Words and Music by ELTON JOHN
and BERNIE TAUPIN

GREEN GREEN GRASS OF HOME

VIOLIN

Words and Music by
CURLY PUTMAN

HAPPY DAYS

Theme from the Paramount Television Series HAPPY DAYS

VIOLIN

Words by NORMAN GIMBEL
Music by CHARLES FOX

HAVE I TOLD YOU LATELY

Violin

Words and Music by
VAN MORRISON

HEART AND SOUL

from the Paramount Short Subject A SONG IS BORN

Words by FRANK LOESSER
Music by HOAGY CARMICHAEL

VIOLIN

HOGAN'S HEROES MARCH
from the Television Series HOGAN'S HEROES

VIOLIN

By JERRY FIELDING

HERE WITHOUT YOU

Violin

Words and Music by MATT ROBERTS,
BRAD ARNOLD, CHRISTOPHER HENDERSON,
and ROBERT HARRELL

I DREAMED A DREAM
from LES MISÉRABLES

Music by CLAUDE-MICHEL SCHÖNBERG
Lyrics by ALAIN BOUBLIL,
JEAN-MARC NATEL and HERBERT KRETZMER

Violin

I HEARD IT THROUGH THE GRAPEVINE

VIOLIN

Words and Music by NORMAN J. WHITFIELD
and BARRETT STRONG

I SAY A LITTLE PRAYER

VIOLIN

Lyric by HAL DAVID
Music by BURT BACHARACH

Moderately fast

I WHISTLE A HAPPY TUNE

from THE KING AND I

VIOLIN

Lyrics by OSCAR HAMMERSTEIN II
Music by RICHARD RODGERS

Brightly

I WILL REMEMBER YOU
Theme from THE BROTHERS McMULLEN

Violin

Words and Music by SARAH McLACHLAN,
SEAMUS EGAN and DAVE MERENDA

I WRITE THE SONGS

VIOLIN

Words and Music by
BRUCE JOHNSTON

Slow Ballad

I'M POPEYE THE SAILOR MAN

Theme from the Paramount Cartoon POPEYE THE SAILOR

VIOLIN

Words and Music by
SAMMY LERNER

IF I EVER LOSE MY FAITH IN YOU

VIOLIN

Music and Lyrics by
STING

IMAGINE

VIOLIN

Words and Music by
JOHN LENNON

Medium slow

IT'S MY LIFE

VIOLIN

Words and Music by JON BON JOVI,
RICHARD SAMBORA and MARTIN SANDBERG

IT'S STILL ROCK AND ROLL TO ME

VIOLIN

Words and Music by
BILLY JOEL

JAILHOUSE ROCK

VIOLIN

Words and Music by JERRY LEIBER
and MIKE STOLLER

JOY TO THE WORLD

VIOLIN

Words and Music by
HOYT AXTON

Moderate Gospel Rock

JUMP, JIVE AN' WAIL

VIOLIN

Words and Music by
LOUIS PRIMA

KANSAS CITY

VIOLIN

Words and Music by JERRY LEIBER
and MIKE STOLLER

KOKOMO
from the Motion Picture COCKTAIL

VIOLIN

Words and Music by MIKE LOVE, TERRY MELCHER,
JOHN PHILLIPS and SCOTT McKENZIE

LET 'EM IN

VIOLIN

Words and Music by
PAUL and LINDA McCARTNEY

Moderately

LET'S STAY TOGETHER

VIOLIN

Words and Music by AL GREEN,
WILLIE MITCHELL and AL JACKSON, JR.

LIKE A ROCK

VIOLIN

Words and Music by
BOB SEGER

D.S. al Coda

CODA

LIVIN' LA VIDA LOCA

VIOLIN

Words and Music by ROBI ROSA
and DESMOND CHILD

LOVE AND MARRIAGE

VIOLIN

Words by SAMMY CAHN
Music by JAMES VAN HEUSEN

LOVE STORY
Theme from the Paramount Picture LOVE STORY

VIOLIN

Music by FRANCIS LAI

MAGGIE MAY

VIOLIN

Words and Music by ROD STEWART
and MARTIN QUITTENTON

MAKING OUR DREAMS COME TRUE
Theme from the Paramount Television Series LAVERNE AND SHIRLEY

VIOLIN

Words by NORMAN GIMBEL
Music by CHARLES FOX

Bright 4

MAYBE I'M AMAZED

VIOLIN

Words and Music by
PAUL McCARTNEY

Moderately

small notes optional

MICHELLE

VIOLIN

Words and Music by JOHN LENNON
and PAUL McCARTNEY

MICKEY MOUSE MARCH

from Walt Disney's THE MICKEY MOUSE CLUB

VIOLIN

Words and Music by
JIMMIE DODD

MISSION: IMPOSSIBLE THEME

from the Paramount Television Series MISSION: IMPOSSIBLE

VIOLIN

By LALO SCHIFRIN

MISTER SANDMAN

VIOLIN

Lyric and Music by
PAT BALLARD

MOON RIVER

from the Paramount Picture BREAKFAST AT TIFFANY'S

Words by JOHNNY MERCER
Music by HENRY MANCINI

VIOLIN

MY HEART WILL GO ON
(Love Theme from 'Titanic')
from the Paramount and Twentieth Century Fox Motion Picture TITANIC

VIOLIN

Music by JAMES HORNER
Lyric by WILL JENNINGS

MY WAY

VIOLIN

English Words by PAUL ANKA
Original French Words by GILLES THIBAULT
Music by JACQUES REVAUX and CLAUDE FRANCOIS

NA NA HEY HEY KISS HIM GOODBYE

VIOLIN

Words and Music by ARTHUR FRASHUER DALE,
PAUL ROGER LEKA and GARY CARLA

ON BROADWAY

VIOLIN

Words and Music by BARRY MANN,
CYNTHIA WEIL, MIKE STOLLER and JERRY LEIBER

PEPPERMINT TWIST

VIOLIN

Words and Music by JOSEPH DiNICOLA
and HENRY GLOVER

POCKETFUL OF MIRACLES

VIOLIN

Words by SAMMY CAHN
Music by JAMES VAN HEUSEN

Moderately, with a lilt

PUFF THE MAGIC DRAGON

VIOLIN

Words and Music by LENNY LIPTON
and PETER YARROW

PUT YOUR HAND IN THE HAND

VIOLIN

Words and Music by
GENE MacLELLAN

QUIET NIGHTS OF QUIET STARS
(Corcovado)

VIOLIN

English Words by GENE LEES
Original Words and Music by ANTONIO CARLOS JOBIM

Moderately slow

ROCK AROUND THE CLOCK

Violin

Words and Music by MAX C. FREEDMAN
and JIMMY DeKNIGHT

ROCK WITH YOU

VIOLIN

Words and Music by
ROD TEMPERTON

SATIN DOLL

VIOLIN

By DUKE ELLINGTON

SAVE THE BEST FOR LAST

Violin

Words and Music by PHIL GALDSTON,
JON LIND and WENDY WALDMAN

Flowing

THEME FROM "SCHINDLER'S LIST"

from the Universal Motion Picture SCHINDLER'S LIST

VIOLIN

Music by JOHN WILLIAMS

SHE WILL BE LOVED

VIOLIN

Words and Music by ADAM LEVINE
and JAMES VALENTINE

SING

from SESAME STREET

Words and Music by
JOE RAPOSO

Violin

SO LONG, FAREWELL
from THE SOUND OF MUSIC

VIOLIN

Lyrics by OSCAR HAMMERSTEIN II
Music by RICHARD RODGERS

SOMEWHERE OUT THERE

from AN AMERICAN TAIL

VIOLIN

Music by BARRY MANN and JAMES HORNER
Lyrics by CYNTHIA WEIL

SPANISH FLEA

VIOLIN

Words and Music by
JULIUS WECHTER

STACY'S MOM

VIOLIN

Words and Music by CHRIS COLLINGWOOD
and ADAM SCHLESINGER

SUNRISE, SUNSET
from the Musical FIDDLER ON THE ROOF

VIOLIN

Words by SHELDON HARNICK
Music by JERRY BOCK

Moderately slow Waltz tempo

TAKE MY BREATH AWAY

(Love Theme)

from the Paramount Picture TOP GUN

VIOLIN

Words and Music by GIORGIO MORODER
and TOM WHITLOCK

Moderately slow

THAT'S AMORÉ
(That's Love)
from the Paramount Picture THE CADDY

Words by JACK BROOKS
Music by HARRY WARREN

VIOLIN

THIS LAND IS YOUR LAND

VIOLIN

Words and Music by
WOODY GUTHRIE

Moderately bright

THOSE WERE THE DAYS

Violin

Words and Music by
GENE RASKIN

TIME AFTER TIME

VIOLIN

Words and Music by CYNDI LAUPER
and ROB HYMAN

Moderately fast Rock

A THOUSAND MILES

VIOLIN

Words and Music by
VANESSA CARLTON

D.C. al Coda

CODA

TOMORROW

from the Musical Production ANNIE

Violin

LYRIC by MARTIN CHARNIN
Music by CHARLES STROUSE

TOP OF THE WORLD

VIOLIN

Words and Music by JOHN BETTIS
and RICHARD CARPENTER

TWIST AND SHOUT

Violin

Words and Music by BERT RUSSELL
and PHIL MEDLEY

UNCHAINED MELODY

Violin

Lyric by HY ZARET
Music by ALEX NORTH

UNDER THE BOARDWALK

VIOLIN

Words and Music by ARTIE RESNICK
and KENNY YOUNG

UNITED WE STAND

Violin

Words and Music by ANTHONY TOBY HILLER
and JOHN GOODISON

THE WAY YOU MOVE

VIOLIN

Words and Music by ANTWAN PATTON,
PATRICK BROWN and CARLTON MAHONE

WE ARE THE WORLD

VIOLIN

Words and Music by LIONEL RICHIE
and MICHAEL JACKSON

WE BELONG TOGETHER

Violin

Words and Music by MARIAH CAREY,
JERMAINE DUPRI, MANUEL SEAL, JOHNTA AUSTIN,
DARNELL BRISTOL, KENNETH EDMONDS, SIDNEY JOHNSON,
PATRICK MOTEN, BOBBY WOMACK and SANDRA SULLY

Slow Soul

To Coda ⊕

D.S. al Coda

CODA ⊕

WHAT THE WORLD NEEDS NOW IS LOVE

VIOLIN

Lyric by HAL DAVID
Music by BURT BACHARACH

WITH A LITTLE HELP FROM MY FRIENDS

VIOLIN

Words and Music by JOHN LENNON
and PAUL McCARTNEY

WONDERFUL TONIGHT

VIOLIN

Words and Music by
ERIC CLAPTON

WOOLY BULLY

Words and Music by
DOMINGO SAMUDIO

VIOLIN

Moderately

small notes optional

YELLOW SUBMARINE

VIOLIN

Words and Music by JOHN LENNON
and PAUL McCARTNEY

YOU ARE THE SUNSHINE OF MY LIFE

VIOLIN

Words and Music by
STEVIE WONDER

YOU RAISE ME UP

VIOLIN

Words and Music by BRENDAN GRAHAM
and ROLF LOVLAND

YOU'VE GOT A FRIEND

VIOLIN

Words and Music by
CAROLE KING

ZIP-A-DEE-DOO-DAH

from Walt Disney's SONG OF THE SOUTH
from Disneyland and Walt Disney World's SPLASH MOUNTAIN

VIOLIN

Words by RAY GILBERT
Music by ALLIE WRUBEL